# USBORNE
# WORLD KITCHEN

Abigail Wheatley

ILLUSTRATED BY
Chaaya Prabhat

RECIPE CONSULTANTS
Maud Eden & Monita Buchwald

DESIGNED BY
Katie Webb

MANAGING DESIGNER
Helen Lee

DIVERSITY CONSULTANTS
Show Racism the Red Card

# USBORNE QUICKLINKS

For links to websites where you can find out how to make food from around the world, find facts about ingredients and where they come from, and watch how-to videos about basic cooking skills, go to **usborne.com/Quicklinks** and type in the title of this book.

You can also download some of the recipes in this book at Usborne Quicklinks, including guidance on how to make them vegan, dairy-free, egg-free, gluten-free and nut-free (or any combination of these).

Please follow the internet safety guidelines at Usborne Quicklinks.
Children should be supervised online.

If you scan this symbol with a smartphone or tablet camera, it will take you to videos that show some basic cooking techniques used in the recipes in this book.

# THANK YOU!

A huge thank you to all the families who made this book possible by contributing their stories and recipes.

# CONTENTS

# GETTING STARTED

This book is full of delicious recipes contributed by families from all around the world. Their recipes are simple enough for beginner cooks and use widely-available ingredients, and equipment you can find at home.

## BEFORE YOU START

Read through the recipe to check you have all the ingredients and equipment you need. Wash your hands – then you're ready to go.

## SERVING SIZES

The recipes in this book are for four people as a light meal or side dish, unless they say otherwise. If you want to make more, double all the ingredients. If you want to make less, halve them.

## FOOD PREFERENCES & ALLERGIES

All of the recipes in this book are vegetarian and can also be made nut-free, gluten-free, egg-free, dairy-free, vegan, or almost any combination of these. For instructions, look for the "Variations" sign on the recipe pages, and on pages 58-61 at the end of the book.

## A PINCH OF SALT

A pinch is the amount you can pick up between your thumb and your first finger. Some recipes include a pinch of salt. Others don't, as there's enough salt in other ingredients such as soy sauce, or cheese.

## MEASURING

It's a good idea to measure ingredients accurately, especially when you're baking cakes or cookies. Small amounts are measured with measuring spoons. The ingredients should lie level with the top of the spoon.

## ASK FOR HELP

Before you use new equipment, or if you're trying out something new, make sure you know what you're doing. If in doubt, ask someone with cooking experience to help you.

## PAN HANDLING

Don't leave pan handles hanging over the front of the stove – turn them to the side, so you don't knock them off. Move hot pans carefully, so you don't spill the contents.

## USING AN OVEN

Cook things on the middle shelf of the oven. Arrange the shelves before you turn on the oven. Some ovens may cook things more quickly or slowly than the recipe says. Set a timer to remind you when to take out your food.

## OVEN MITTS

Food and equipment can get very hot. Protect your hands with oven mitts especially when you're getting things in and out of the oven.

## KEEP WATCH

Don't leave the kitchen while you've got anything cooking on the stove. Make sure you remember to turn off the heat when you've finished.

## TIDY UP

It's a good idea to wipe up any spills on the floor as you go, so you don't slip. If you keep the kitchen fairly tidy as you cook, it makes it easier to keep track of where you're up to, and helps when it comes to cleaning up afterwards.

## CHOP SAFELY

When you're cutting with a sharp knife, use a chopping board to stop food from slipping. The recipe will tell you the safest way to cut things – or look at pages 6-7 for instructions on how to prepare some common ingredients.

# COOKING BASICS

On these pages you'll find tips and techniques showing you how to do some common tasks mentioned in the recipes in this book. You can also watch how-to videos of all these techniques online – just follow the links on page 2 of this book.

## WHIPPING CREAM

1 Pour the cream into a large bowl. If you're using a hand whisk, move it around and around in the cream very quickly.

2 If you're using an electric mixer, turn it to cream-whipping speed.

3 Lift up the whisk or mixer. The cream should stand up in a floppy point. If you whisk too much, the cream will become hard.

## PREPARING ONIONS

1 Cut off the top and root, and peel off the papery skin. Cut the onion in half.

2 Put each half flat side down and cut into thin slices.

3 Cut each slice into tiny pieces.

## PREPARING GARLIC

1 Peel off the papery skin.

2 Crush the garlic in a garlic crusher.

## CRACKING EGGS

1 Crack the egg sharply on the edge of a cup.

2 Push your thumbs into the crack and pull the shell apart.

3 Let the yolk and white slide gently out.

## PREPARING POTATOES

1 Wash the potatoes and cut out any spots.

2 Cut the potatoes into slices, then into bite-sized pieces.

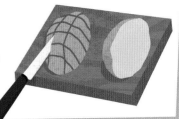

## PREPARING APPLES & PEARS

1 Cut each fruit in half. Put the halves flat side down and cut in half again.

2 To remove the cores, cut away from you, at a slant, to halfway under the core.

3 Turn the piece around and make another cut in the same way.

## PREPARING BELL PEPPERS

1 Press with your thumbs on either side of the stalk, until it pops in.

2 Tear the pepper apart. Throw away the stalk, seeds and white parts.

## GREASING PANS

1 Dip a paper towel in some butter or spread. Wipe it around inside the pan.

## LINING DEEP PANS OR CONTAINERS

1 Put the pan on baking paper like this. Draw around it, then cut across the whole strip.

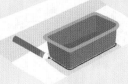

2 Rotate the pan like this, put it on more baking paper, draw around it and cut across the strip.

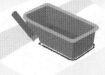

3 Put the thin strip in the bottom of the pan with its ends sticking up. Lay the wide strip on top.

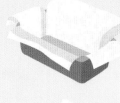

4 For a square container, the strips are the same width. Put one on top of the other.

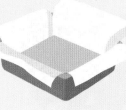

## LINING SHALLOW PANS OR TRAYS

1 Put the pan or tray on baking paper and draw around it.

2 Snip out the shape, cutting just inside the line.

3 Put the shape in the bottom of the pan or tray.

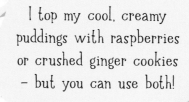

I top my cool, creamy puddings with raspberries or crushed ginger cookies – but you can use both!

Danica's jam cookies
**GERMANY**

Ruth's milk & honey pudding
**SCOTLAND**

Basile's picnic loaf
**FRANCE**

# NORTH AMERICA

Sandra's hot chocolate
**SPAIN**

Marlee's chocolate chip cookies
**USA**

Irene's chicche
**ITALY**

Ikram's kesra bread
**ALGERIA**

My crisp, chewy cookies are so popular that my family members sneak them from the pantry, and fight over the last one!

Isla & Olive's fried rice
**JAMAICA**

My yummy dumplings are made using ricotta cheese and spinach.

# SOUTH AMERICA

Sharon's "Red Red" peas
**GHANA**

Beatriz's "brigadeiro" truffles
**BRAZIL**

I love to help my Auntie cook these black-eyed peas in a rich, red sauce on Saturday mornings.

I make these chocolatey truffles with my sister Fernanda and our Mami (mother), for parties and sleepovers.

Pamela's fruit salad
**ARGENTINA**

My refreshing fruit salad with a creamy sauce is really cooling to eat on hot days – perfect for after a barbecue.

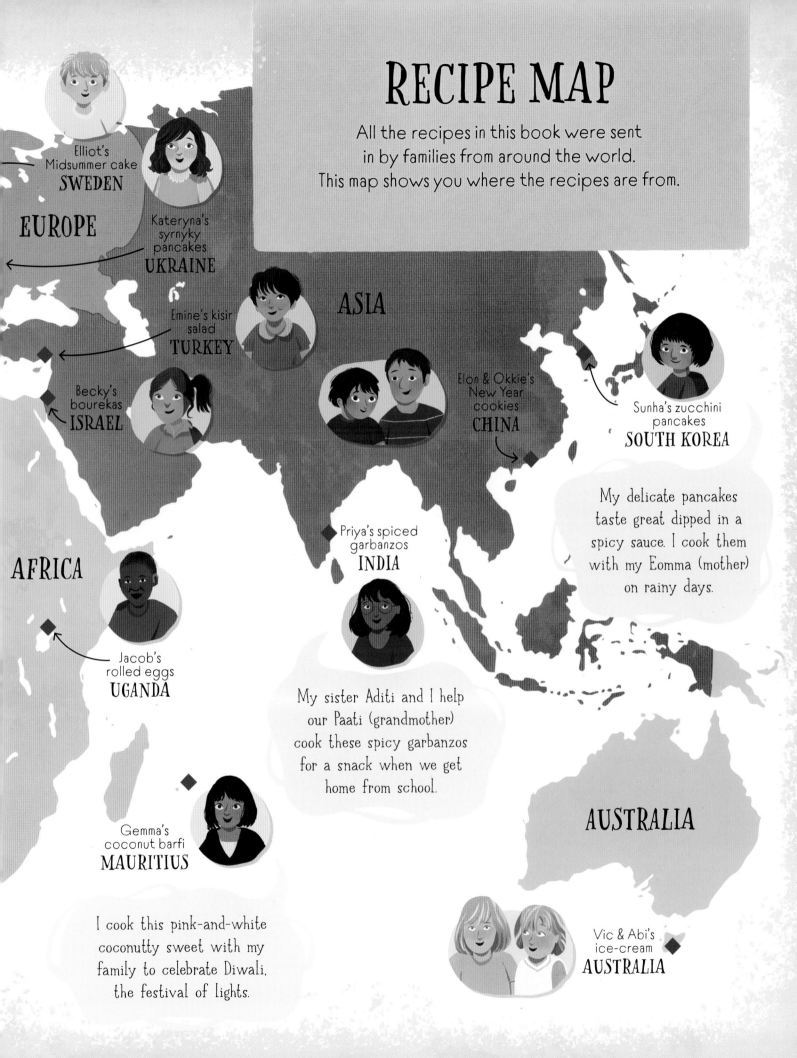

# RECIPE MAP

All the recipes in this book were sent
in by families from around the world.
This map shows you where the recipes are from.

Elliot's
Midsummer cake
**SWEDEN**

**EUROPE**

Kateryna's
syrnyky
pancakes
**UKRAINE**

**ASIA**

Emine's kisir
salad
**TURKEY**

Becky's
bourekas
**ISRAEL**

Elon & Okkie's
New Year
cookies
**CHINA**

Sunha's zucchini
pancakes
**SOUTH KOREA**

My delicate pancakes
taste great dipped in a
spicy sauce. I cook them
with my Eomma (mother)
on rainy days.

Priya's spiced
garbanzos
**INDIA**

**AFRICA**

Jacob's
rolled eggs
**UGANDA**

My sister Aditi and I help
our Paati (grandmother)
cook these spicy garbanzos
for a snack when we get
home from school.

**AUSTRALIA**

Gemma's
coconut barfi
**MAURITIUS**

I cook this pink-and-white
coconutty sweet with my
family to celebrate Diwali,
the festival of lights.

Vic & Abi's
ice-cream
**AUSTRALIA**

9

# SUNHA'S ZUCCHINI PANCAKES

Hi, I'm Sunha and I'm from South Korea. When I was small my Eomma (mother) cooked this recipe with me on rainy days, using zucchini from our backyard. When a delicate pancake was cooked, Eomma tore off a piece and popped it into my mouth.

This is a Korean variety of zucchini called *aehobak*, but the recipe is also delicious made with ordinary zucchini.

## INGREDIENTS

For the pancakes:

- 1 large zucchini
- ½ cup all-purpose flour
- ¼ cup cold water
- a pinch of salt
- 2 tablespoons sunflower oil or other light cooking oil
- 1 tablespoon sesame oil (optional)

For the dipping sauce:

- 1 small clove of garlic
- 2 tablespoons soy sauce
- 1 tablespoon rice wine vinegar or white wine vinegar
- a pinch of dried chili flakes (optional)

You will also need a medium or large non-stick frying pan.

**1** Wash and shred the zucchini.

Measure the shredded zucchini – you will need $3\frac{1}{4}$ cups.

Grater

Big holes

**2** Squeeze the shredded zucchini over a sink.

Get out as much liquid as you can.

**3** Put the zucchini in a big bowl.

Add the flour, water and salt, and mix well.

This is the pancake mix.

**4** Mix the sunflower and sesame oil. Spoon a tablespoon into the pan. Put over medium heat for 2-3 minutes.

Scoop up a heaping tablespoonful of pancake mix. Squash it down into the spoon. Tip it into the pan.

SIZZLE

**5** Add more spoonfuls of the pancake mix, leaving gaps between. Cook for 2-3 minutes.

Turn over. Cook for 2-3 minutes more.

FLIP

**6** When the edges turn golden-brown, lift the pancakes onto a plate.

Add more oil and pancake mix. Cook as before, until the pancake mix is used up.

Cover with an upside-down plate to keep them warm.

**7** For the sauce, peel the papery skin off the garlic. Crush the garlic and mix it with the soy sauce, vinegar and chili flakes.

Small bowl

**8** Dip a piece of pancake into the sauce. Then eat!

Mmm!

# VARIATIONS

To make this recipe gluten-free, use gluten-free flour and gluten-free "tamari" soy sauce.

To make it sesame-free, leave out the sesame oil.

The dipping sauce is spicy – leave out the chili if you like.

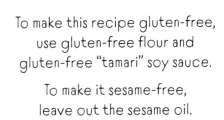

# EMINE'S KISIR SALAD

Hello, my name is Emine and I'm from Turkey. As a child, my favorite recipe was kisir – a spicy salad made using bulgur wheat, a grain also known as cracked wheat. It's important to use bulgur wheat marked "fine," as the ordinary type won't cook in the same way. When I saw my Anne (mother) making kisir, I was always excited, as it meant family and friends were coming to visit!

Kisir is often decorated with seeds from pomegranates – a type of fruit that grows in many Turkish gardens.

If you can't get some of the ingredients, you'll find alternatives under "Variations."

# INGREDIENTS

- 1 cup fine bulgur wheat, or couscous
- 1 cup hot water
- ½ onion
- 1 clove of garlic
- 2 teaspoons olive oil
- 1½ tablespoons tomato paste
- 1 lemon
- 2 scallions

- a small handful of fresh flat-leaf parsley
- 1½ teaspoons ground cumin
- 1½ teaspoons sumac (see "Variations" for alternatives)
- ½ teaspoon Turkish "Urfa" chili, or dried chili flakes
- a pinch of salt
- 1 tablespoon pomegranate molasses (see "Variations" for alternatives)
- 2 Romaine lettuce hearts
- 1 pomegranate (optional)

**1** Put the bulgur wheat or couscous in a heat-proof bowl. Pour on the hot water.

Cover the bowl with a plate and leave for 15 minutes.

**2** Meanwhile, peel the papery skin off the onion and garlic. Cut the onion into small pieces and crush the garlic.

The instructions on page 6 will help you.

**3** Put the oil in a frying pan over medium heat. After 2 minutes, add the onion.

Cook for 3 minutes, stirring now and then.

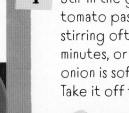

**4** Stir in the garlic and tomato paste. Cook, stirring often, for 3 minutes, or until the onion is soft. Take it off the heat.

STIR

**5** Cut the lemon in half.

Squeeze out the juice.

Citrus squeezer

**6** Snip the roots and dark green parts off the scallions and throw them away.

Snip the rest into small pieces.

**7** Pull the parsley leaves off the stalks. Put the leaves in a mug.

Snip them up.

Scissors

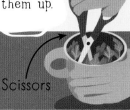

**8** Put the cooked onion mixture, lemon juice, scallions and parsley in the bowl with the bulgur. Add the cumin, sumac, chili, salt and molasses.

Stir. Leave to cool for 20 minutes.

**9** Meanwhile, separate the lettuce leaves so they stay whole.

Cut the pomegranate into quarters. Ease out the red seeds carefully, as the juice can stain!

**10** Fill each leaf with the bulgur mixture. Sprinkle over some pomegranate seeds.

## VARIATIONS

If you don't have sumac, grate the yellow zest from half a lemon on the small holes of a grater. Add 1 teaspoon of zest at step 8.

If you don't have pomegranate molasses, squeeze the juice from half a lemon and mix with 1 teaspoon of sugar. Add at step 8.

To make this recipe gluten-free, you will need 1 cup quinoa instead of the bulgur. See page 58 for instructions.

13

# FRUITS AND VEGETABLES

Our world is home to an astonishing variety of colorful and delicious fruits and vegetables. Some, such as bananas and potatoes, are familiar almost everywhere, while others may only be known in a few regions or countries.

**ZUCCHINI** come in many shapes, colors and sizes and go well with savory flavors. Zucchini were first grown in Italy, but are now much loved in many countries.

*The South Korean pancake recipe on page 10 uses zucchini.*

**BEETS** are root vegetables with an earthy, slightly sweet taste. They're popular in the UK, Germany, Sweden, Poland, Ukraine and India. Most beets are pinkish-purple, but there are also colorful and even striped varieties.

A fruit called **FINGER LIME** comes from Australia and grows in many different colors. It tastes similar to ordinary limes, but its long, thin fruits contain tiny, juicy blobs or "pearls."

14

**UQA** or **OCA** are underground stems (or tubers) popular as a vegetable in Argentina, Bolivia, Venezuela, Peru and New Zealand. Traditionally the tubers are red, but other colors are also grown.

**POMEGRANATE** fruit have a hard outer case filled with juicy red seeds that have a sweet but sharp flavor. Pomegranates are popular in many parts of the world.

*Use pomegranate seeds in the kisir salad on page 12.*

**PLANTAIN** is a fruit related to bananas that's eaten as a vegetable. It's loved across West and Central Africa, the Caribbean and Central and South America and can be fried, boiled, roasted, or made into flour.

**PAK CHOI** or **BOK CHOY** is a leafy green vegetable that started off in Asia but is now well known around the world. The crisp, juicy stems taste mild and sweet while the leaves are slightly bitter.

15

# BECKY'S BOUREKAS

Hi, I'm Becky. Every summer in my childhood I visited my Safta (grandmother) in Israel. With the help of Safta's treasured rolling pin, we cooked bourekas – little puffy pastries topped with crunchy sesame seeds.

Bourekas can have different shapes and fillings. These are triangles, filled with feta cheese.

MEOW

# INGREDIENTS

- a medium potato
- 1 large egg
- 4oz feta cheese (around 1 cup crumbled)
- a pinch of black pepper
- 1 store-bought frozen puff pastry sheet
- 2 tablespoons black or white sesame seeds, or a mixture of both (optional)

You will also need a large baking tray.

MAKES
9

TIP

Before you start, leave the pastry at room temperature for 30 minutes.

**1** Cut the potato into small pieces (page 6). Put in a pan. Cover with cold water. Put over medium heat.

**2** When the water boils, turn down the heat so it bubbles gently. Put on a lid, leaving a small gap. Cook for 10-15 minutes.

Then poke with a knife to check they're soft.

**3** Drain in a sieve over a sink, then mash until smooth.

Masher

Big bowl

MASH

**4** Crack the egg (page 6). Mix the yolk and white.

Fork

Cup

**5** Add half the egg (save the rest for later). Crumble in the feta. Add the pepper.

Mix well.

This is the filling.

**6** Line the tray – see page 7 for instructions. Heat the oven to 375°F.

Baking paper

**7** Dust a surface and rolling pin with flour. Unroll the pastry.

Roll lightly to stretch the pastry into a square.

ROLL

**8** Snip the pastry into 9 squares. Put a teaspoon of filling on each.

**9** Fold each diagonally to make a triangle.

Press the edges together with a finger, then a fork. Put on the tray.

PRESS

**10** Brush the remaining egg over the tops.

Pastry brush

**11** Scatter the seeds over the top. Bake for 20-25 minutes, until golden-brown. Leave on the trays to cool.

# VARIATIONS

To make this recipe egg-free, dairy-free, vegan, gluten-free or sesame-free, see page 58 for instructions.

# ELON & OKKIE'S NEW YEAR COOKIES

Hi, we're Elon and Okkie. We love baking these cookies at Chinese New Year with our Por Por and Gung Gung (grandmother and grandfather), who come from Hong Kong in China. We celebrate by decorating the house, dressing up in red and sharing delicious food.

*Our cookies have a crunchy coating of sesame seeds...*

*...but if you don't eat sesame, look at "Variations" opposite.*

**1** Heat the oven to 375°F. Line the tray – see page 7 for instructions.

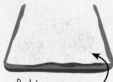

Baking paper

**2** Put a sieve over a big bowl. Put in the flour, cornstarch and baking powder.

*Tap until they go through.*

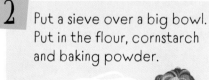

**3** Add the sugar, salt, oil and water.

*Mix well.*

**4** Use your hands to squish the mixture into a lump of dough.

**5** Pull the dough into two equal parts. Pull each part in half again.

**6** Then, divide each of these parts into four equal pieces.

*You will have 16 pieces.*

**7** Put the sesame seeds in a small, shallow bowl.

# INGREDIENTS

- 1 cup all-purpose flour
- 3 tablespoons cornstarch
- ½ teaspoon baking powder
- 3 tablespoons sugar
- a pinch of salt
- 3 tablespoons sunflower oil or other light cooking oil
- 2 tablespoons water
- 3 tablespoons sesame seeds (optional)

You will also need a baking tray.

**MAKES 16**

**8** Roll each piece of dough between your palms to make a ball.

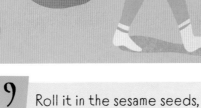

**9** Roll it in the sesame seeds, then put it on the tray.

Roll and coat each piece of dough in the same way.

**10** Put the tray in the oven.

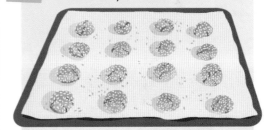

Bake for 12-15 minutes until golden-brown. Cool on the tray.

# VARIATIONS

To make this recipe gluten-free, use gluten-free flour.

Instead of sesame seeds, you could use granulated sugar or shredded coconut.

# RUTH'S MILK & HONEY PUDDING

Hello, I'm Ruth. Every summer when I was little I visited my Auntie Chrissie in her farmhouse on the Isle of Mull in Scotland. Together we milked Daisy the cow, then we used the creamy milk to make this pudding, and decorated it with wild raspberries.

The pudding is set firm using carrageen, a local type of seaweed...

...but you can buy "vegetarian gelatin" which is made from carrageen and is flavorless.

## INGREDIENTS

For the puddings:

- 1 cup full-fat milk
- 1 cup heavy or whipping cream
- 2 tablespoons honey
- ½ teaspoon vegetarian gelatin

For the topping:

- a handful of fresh raspberries OR
- 3 store-bought ginger snap cookies

You will also need four small bowls or cups.

MAKES 4

**1** Pour the milk, cream and honey into a small saucepan.

Stir, then sprinkle over the vegetarian gelatin.

**2** Put the pan over gentle heat.

Stir all the time, until bubbles form at the edge.

**3** Leave it to bubble for 30 seconds, then take it off the heat.

Pour it into the glasses, cups or bowls.

Ladle

POUR

**4** Leave until cold, then refrigerate for one hour.

**5** Leave the puddings in their containers – or, to turn them out...

...use a finger to pull the edge away from the container...

...then hold upside down over a plate and shake.

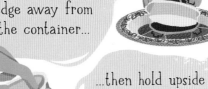

**6** For the topping, we use raspberries or ginger snap cookies...

...but you can use both if you like!

**7** If you're using ginger snaps, wrap in a cloth dishtowel, then tap with a rolling pin to crush them into crumbs.

Sprinkle them over the puddings.

CRUNCH

**8** Scatter on the raspberries, if you're using them.

## VARIATIONS

To make this recipe dairy-free, vegan or gluten-free, follow the instructions on page 59.

21

# COOKING TOOLS

Cooks across the globe use many different types of cooking tools, or utensils – from a humble wooden spoon to knives designed for specialist tasks. On these pages you'll find out about some interesting tools from around the world.

Lots of people use **ROLLING PINS** to roll out dough, pastry or other things into an even layer. Rolling pins can be made of materials such as wood, plastic, metal or stone, and come in many shapes and sizes.

*Use a rolling pin in the recipes on pages 16, 20, 48 and 52.*

This **IJABE**, or blending broomstick, is from Nigeria. It's made from palm tree stalks and is used to mash and blend cooked foods to a smooth purée.

A **DAO BAO** or **CAI BAO** is a knife from Vietnam with a leaf-shaped blade and central slit. The blade is for slicing fruit and vegetables, while the slit is for shredding them.

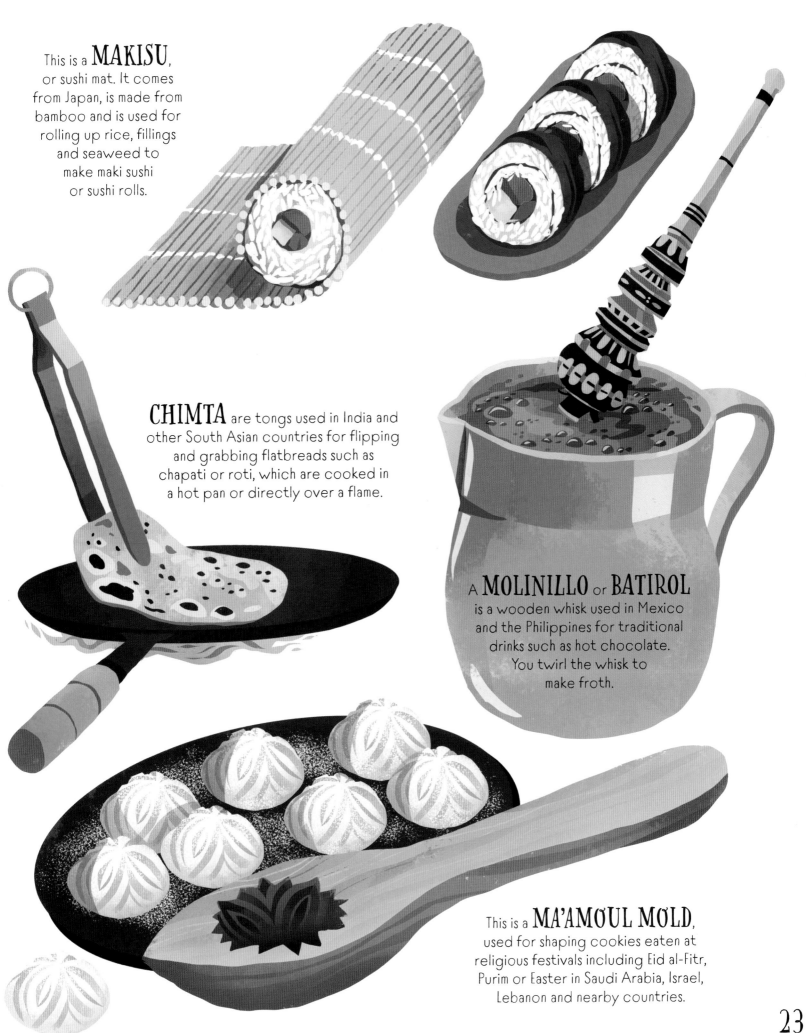

This is a **MAKISU**, or sushi mat. It comes from Japan, is made from bamboo and is used for rolling up rice, fillings and seaweed to make maki sushi or sushi rolls.

**CHIMTA** are tongs used in India and other South Asian countries for flipping and grabbing flatbreads such as chapati or roti, which are cooked in a hot pan or directly over a flame.

A **MOLINILLO** or **BATIROL** is a wooden whisk used in Mexico and the Philippines for traditional drinks such as hot chocolate. You twirl the whisk to make froth.

This is a **MA'AMOUL MOLD**, used for shaping cookies eaten at religious festivals including Eid al-Fitr, Purim or Easter in Saudi Arabia, Israel, Lebanon and nearby countries.

23

# SHARON'S "RED RED" PEAS

Hello, I'm Sharon and I'm from Ghana. When I was growing up, on Saturday mornings my Naana (grandmother) took me to the local market, where we visited my Auntie's Chop Bar (restaurant). Sometimes my Auntie let me help prepare my favorite dish, "Red Red," which includes stewed black-eyed peas in a rich, red sauce.

"Red Red" peas are served with a fried fruit called plantain and "garri" flakes made from the cassava plant. But the peas are also delicious on their own, or served alongside other food.

The traditional cooking oil is red palm oil, but you can use other vegetable oils instead, such as olive or sunflower.

## INGREDIENTS

- 1 small onion
- 1 large tomato
- a 1 inch long piece of fresh ginger
- 2 cloves of garlic
- 2 scallions
- a vegetable stock cube
- 1⅔ cups hot water
- 2 tablespoons cooking oil such as olive, sunflower or red palm oil

- 4 tablespoons tomato paste
- 2 teaspoons paprika
- 2 x 15oz cans black-eyed peas (or black beans)
- a pinch of ground black pepper
- a fresh red chili, or a pinch of dried chili flakes (optional)

You will also need a large non-stick pan.

**1** Take the skin off the onion, then cut the onion into small pieces.

The instructions on page 6 will help you.

**2** Cut the tomato in half, then into quarters, and then into small pieces.

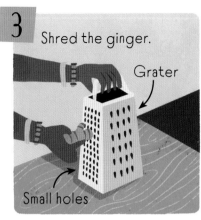

SLICE

**3** Shred the ginger.

Grater

Small holes

**4** Peel the papery skin off the garlic.

Crush the garlic.

Garlic crusher

**5** Snip the roots and dark green parts off the scallions and throw them away. Snip the rest into small bits.

SNIP

**6** Crumble the stock cube into a measuring cup. Add the hot water.

Stir well.

**7** Heat the oil in the pan over medium heat for around 30 seconds.

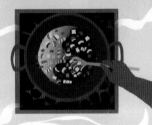

Add the onion. Cook for 3-4 minutes, stirring regularly.

**8** Add the tomato, ginger, garlic, tomato paste and paprika. Cook for 1 minute, stirring all the time.

**9** Pour in the stock. Wait until it bubbles. Turn down the heat so it's bubbling gently.

Cook for 10 minutes, stirring now and then.

**10** Pour in the black-eyed peas and can liquid.

Add the scallions, pepper and chili. Stir, and turn up the heat a little.

**11** Wait until it bubbles. Turn down the heat so it bubbles gently.

Cook for 15 minutes, stirring now and then. If you used a fresh chili, take it out.

## VARIATIONS

To make this recipe gluten-free, use a gluten-free stock cube.

This recipe is just a little spicy, but you can leave out the chili if you prefer.

# ELLIOT'S MIDSUMMER CAKE

Hej! My name is Elliot and I love to cook with my Mamma, who's from Sweden. This recipe is for a layer cake with strawberry-and-cream frosting that we bake to celebrate Midsummer – our most important festival. We make decorations from leaves and flowers and meet friends and family outdoors for games and a picnic.

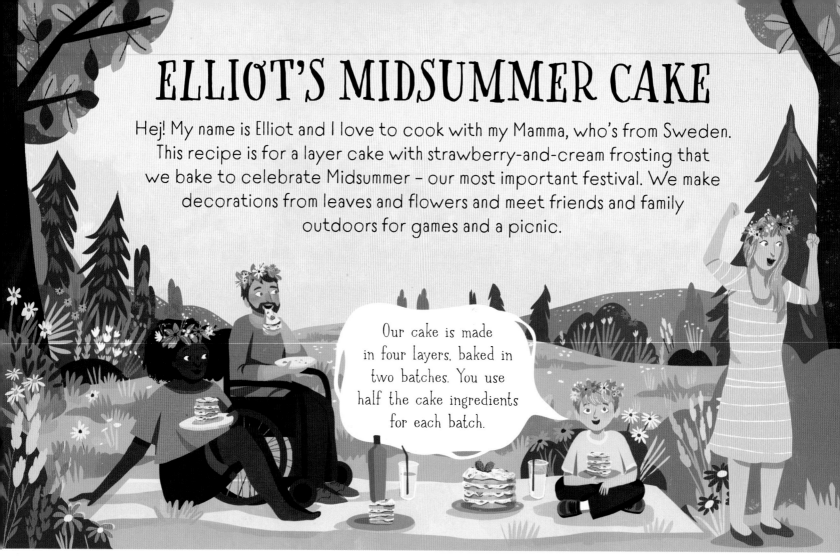

Our cake is made in four layers, baked in two batches. You use half the cake ingredients for each batch.

**1** Heat the oven to 350°F. Grease and line the pans – see page 7 for instructions.

Baking paper

**2** Crack two eggs into a big bowl (page 6.) Add ½ cup of the sugar and ½ teaspoon of the vanilla.

Use a whisk or electric mixer to beat hard for 5 minutes, until thick and pale.

**3** Put 1 cup + 2 tablespoons of the flour, 2½ teaspoons of the baking powder and ½ teaspoon of the cream of tartar in a sieve over a big bowl. Tap the sieve so it all falls through.

Stir gently until just mixed in.

STIR

**4** Divide the mixture between the pans. Spread it out in a thin layer, right to the edges.

Then, bake for 12-15 minutes.

**5** Poke the middle with your finger. If it feels firm and springy, it's cooked.

POKE

If not, bake for 5 minutes more, then test again.

**6** Leave to cool for 10 minutes. Then, run a blunt knife around the edge of each pan.

Turn upside down and shake. Peel off the paper.

# INGREDIENTS

**For the cake:**

- 4 large eggs
- 1 cup granulated sugar
- 1 teaspoon vanilla extract
- 2 cups + 4 tablespoons all-purpose flour
- 5 teaspoons baking powder
- 1 teaspoon cream of tartar

**For the frosting:**

- 1 x 4oz package full-fat cream cheese
- 1 cup powdered sugar
- 1 cup heavy or whipping cream
- 11oz strawberries (around 2 cups when cut)

You will also need two 8-inch round cake pans.

## VARIATIONS

To make this recipe gluten-free, dairy-free, egg-free and/or vegan, follow the instructions on page 59.

**7** Wash and dry the pans, then grease and line them (page 7.)

Repeat steps 2-6 again to make two more cakes.

**8** For the frosting, put the cream cheese in a big bowl.

Sift in the powdered sugar. Beat until smooth.

**TAP TAP**

**9** Whisk in the cream a little at a time. Whisk until the mixture stands up in a soft point like this.

Use a hand whisk or electric mixer.

**10** Set aside three strawberries. Remove the green leaves from the others. Snip the strawberries into small pieces. Mix them in.

**SNIP**

**11** Put a cake on a plate. Spread on a quarter of the frosting. Put on another cake. Spread on another quarter of frosting. Repeat with the other cakes and frosting.

Top with the whole strawberries.

# PAMELA'S FRUIT SALAD

I'm Pamela and I come from a seaside city in Argentina. My favorite recipe is for fruit salad – my Abuelita (grandmother) taught me how to make it when I was small. We always ate it on hot days after a barbecue. For parties, we made a sweet sauce for our fruit salad.

## INGREDIENTS

**For the fruit salad:**

- 1 orange
- 1 banana
- a small handful of black grapes
- a small handful of strawberries
- 1 red apple
- 1 ripe pear
- a can of peaches in juice
- 2 cups of cold orange juice

**For the sauce:**

- 3 tablespoons sweetened condensed milk
- 2 tablespoons Greek-style yogurt

> We sometimes swap in different fruit – but we ALWAYS include canned peaches!

**1** Peel the orange and banana. Wash the grapes, strawberries, apple and pear and pull off stalks and leaves. Drain a handful of peaches.

**2** Cut the apple and pear into quarters and cut out the cores – see page 7.

SLICE

**3** Cut all the fruit into bite-sized pieces, then put in a big bowl. Pour over the orange juice.

> Mix, then spoon into small bowls.

**4** For the sauce, mix the condensed milk and yogurt in a small bowl. Spoon a little sauce on before eating.

MIX

## VARIATIONS

To make this recipe dairy-free or vegan, follow the instructions on page 59.

28

# VIC & ABI'S ICE-CREAM

Hi! We're Vic and Abi, and we're Australian. When we were little, we loved to help our Mum make this yummy vanilla ice-cream – she learned the recipe from her mum. For special occasions such as birthdays, we made our ice-cream the day before, then ate it for breakfast in the garden.

This ice-cream is delicious with fresh fruit. We use passionfruit from our garden, but you can use other fruit.

## INGREDIENTS

- 7oz or ½ can sweetened condensed milk
- 2 cups heavy or whipping cream
- 1 teaspoon vanilla extract

You will also need a freezer-proof lidded food container that holds around 1 quart.

**1** Put the condensed milk, cream and vanilla in a big bowl.

Use a hand whisk or electric mixer to beat the mixture. Keep on for around 3 minutes.

**2** Lift up the whisk. The mixture should stand up in a soft peak below the whisk.

If not, then whisk more and test again.

**3** Scrape the mixture into the container. Put on the lid.

Freeze for 8-10 hours, or overnight.

**4** When you want to eat the ice-cream, leave the container at room temperature for 5 minutes before scooping it.

## VARIATIONS

To make this recipe dairy-free or vegan, use ½ can of plant-based condensed "milk," and plant-based whipping "cream."

29

# JACOB'S ROLLED EGGS

Hello, my name's Jacob. I learned this recipe from my Uncle Senti, who's from Uganda. It's called "rolled eggs" because it's an egg omelet rolled up in a wrap. In Uganda, it's a popular street food, but when I visit Uncle Senti, we make it at home. It's not traditional, but I like to dip my rolled eggs in ketchup!

In Uganda people use a type of wrap called a chapati for rolled eggs.

You can buy chapatis (they may crack a little when you roll them up) or use a soft wrap instead.

# INGREDIENTS

**For the rolled eggs:**
- a small piece of cabbage
- 2 scallions
- a handful of fresh cilantro leaves
- 1 medium-sized tomato
- 4 large eggs
- a pinch of dried chili flakes
- a pinch of salt
- a pinch of ground black pepper
- 2 tablespoons cooking oil such as sunflower
- 2 chapatis or soft wraps

**For dipping:**
- 2 tablespoons mayonnaise
- 2 tablespoons mango chutney
- OR some ketchup if you prefer!

You will also need a non-stick frying pan the same size as your chapatis or wraps, and a pan lid or heatproof plate that fits over the frying pan.

**1** Shred the cabbage into thin strips...

Stop when you have ²/₃ of a cup.

**2** Snip off the roots and dark green parts of the scallions and throw them away.

Snip the rest into small pieces.

**3** Put the cilantro leaves in a cup.

Snip into tiny pieces.

Scissors

**4** Cut the tomato into small pieces.

SLICE

**5** Crack the eggs into a big cup (see page 6).

**6** Mix the yolks and whites.

Then mix in the cabbage, scallions, cilantro, tomato and chili, salt and pepper.

**7** Put one tablespoon of the oil in the frying pan.

Put the pan over medium heat.

**8** Pour in half the egg mixture.

Turn the heat to medium/low and cover with the lid or heatproof plate.

**9** Cook for around 5 minutes, or until the egg is firm on top, and turn off the heat.

Put the wrap on top and cover again, then leave for 5 minutes.

**10** Mix the mayonnaise and mango chutney.

Small bowl

MIX

**11** If you used a lid, take it off and put on an upturned plate.

Carefully turn over the pan and plate, then take off the pan.

**12** Cover with another plate. Then, repeat steps 7, 8, 9 and 11 to make a second one.

**13** Roll up the wraps with the omelets inside. Cut each roll in half.

Dip into the sauce as you eat.

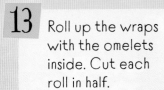

# VARIATIONS

To make this recipe gluten-free, use a gluten-free wrap.

To make the recipe egg-free or vegan, follow the instructions on page 60.

31

# FESTIVE FOOD

All around the world, people love to celebrate special occasions by sharing food with family and friends. Each region has its own festive food traditions. Here are just a handful of celebratory dishes, but you'll find more featured on the recipe pages of this book.

A coconutty sweet called **BARFI** is made to celebrate Diwali, the festival of lights, in Mauritius, India, Fiji, the Caribbean and parts of eastern Africa. It's decorated with nuts, sugar sprinkles, or sometimes real gold or silver.

*Find a barfi recipe from Mauritius on page 34.*

In Romania, **PASCA** bread is popular at Easter and other celebrations such as weddings. It's made from sweet dough braided into a circle, with a cheesecake-like mixture in the middle.

In Hungary at Christmas, people make a cake called **BEIGLI**, that's rolled around a poppy seed or walnut filling and then cut into slices. Similar cakes are popular in Poland, Latvia, Romania, Slovakia, Serbia and Bosnia.

*For another recipe enjoyed at Christmas, see page 36.*

32

In Indonesia, **KETUPAT** is a dish made of rice cooked inside a woven palm leaf package. It's eaten, along with other foods such as soups or spicy stews, at Islamic holidays Eid al-Fitr and Eid al-Adha.

**MEGHLI**, or **KARAWIYAH**, is a sweet, spiced rice pudding decorated with nuts. It's eaten in Lebanon, Palestine, Syria and Jordan to celebrate the birth of a new baby.

**PUMPKIN PIE** is made in Canada and the U.S.A. at Thanksgiving, a holiday to celebrate a good harvest of food. The pie has a pastry crust with a sweet pumpkin filling.

**THUNG TONG**, or "gold bags," are crispy parcels filled with meat and vegetables. Some families exchange them to wish each other good fortune at Songkran, a New Year festival celebrated in Thailand.

# GEMMA'S COCONUT BARFI

Hello, I'm Gemma and I'm from the Indian Ocean island of Mauritius. When I was growing up I made this recipe every year with my family for Diwali, the festival of lights. We decorated our home and shared sweets such as this barfi – a type of fudge made with coconut.

This recipe uses ghee – it's a special type of butter. But you can use ordinary butter or plant-based spread instead.

## INGREDIENTS

- 3 cups unsweetened shredded coconut
- a 14oz can of sweetened condensed milk
- ¼ teaspoon ground cardamom (optional)
- 2½ teaspoons ghee, butter or spread
- a little pink food dye

For topping (optional):

- sugar sprinkles OR
- chopped pistachio nuts (avoid using nuts for anyone who has a nut allergy)

You will also need a food container measuring around 7x7 inches.

**MAKES AROUND 25 PIECES**

34

**1** Line the food container.

See the instructions on page 7.

Baking paper

**2** Put the coconut in a saucepan, over medium heat.

Cook for around a minute, stirring all the time, until it turns pale brown.

**3** Stir in the condensed milk.

The coconut will quickly soak it all up.

**4** Mix in the cardamom and ghee, butter or spread. Keep stirring for around 5 minutes. The mixture will thicken and clump together.

Take the pan off the heat.

**5** Spoon half the mixture into the container. Press it flat using a flexible spatula.

PRESS

**6** Mix a few drops of pink food dye into the remaining mixture in the pan.

Smooth the pink mixture into the lined container, too.

**7** If you'd like to add toppings, sprinkle them on and press them down with the back of a spoon.

Then, refrigerate for one hour.

**8** Remove from the container.

Use a sharp knife to cut the barfi into squares or diamonds.

SLICE

# VARIATIONS

To make this recipe dairy-free, use plant-based condensed "milk," and plant-based spread.

To make it vegan, make it dairy-free as above, and use plant-based sprinkles or pistachios.

To make it nut-free, use sprinkles instead of pistachios.

# ISLA & OLIVE'S FRIED RICE

Hello, we're sisters and our recipe is for fried rice, flavored with spices and a squeeze of lime juice. We learned it from our Grandma - she loves cooking dishes from Jamaica, where our Grandad grew up. We and our cousins Asher and Cohen really look forward to eating this when the family gets together at Christmas. It's such an exciting moment, when Grandma carries the bowl to the table!

If you don't like spicy food, leave out the chili and paprika – the other spices aren't hot, they just add flavor.

This fried rice makes a side dish for around 6 people, or you can make it into an entrée – see "Variations" on the page opposite.

## INGREDIENTS

- 1 large onion
- 2 large cloves of garlic
- 1 red bell pepper
- 1 green bell pepper
- 2 limes
- 4 tablespoons vegetable oil
- 1 teaspoon dried thyme
- 1 tablespoon ground turmeric

- 1 teaspoon ground allspice
- 1 teaspoon ground cumin
- a pinch of salt and a pinch of ground black pepper
- 2 teaspoons ground paprika (optional)
- a pinch of chili powder (optional)
- 2 x 8½oz packages ready-cooked basmati rice

You will also need a large non-stick pan.

**1** Take the skin off the onion, then cut the onion into small pieces.

The instructions on page 6 will help you.

**2** Peel the papery skin off the garlic.

Crush the garlic.

Garlic crusher

**3** Prepare the bell peppers – see page 7 for instructions.

Then cut them into pieces.

**4** Cut the limes in half. Squeeze out the juice.

SQUEEZE

Citrus squeezer

**5** Put the frying pan over medium heat. Add the oil. After 1 minute, add the onion and garlic. Cook for 3 minutes.

Stir now and then.

**6** Add the bell peppers, thyme, turmeric, allspice, cumin, salt, black pepper, paprika and chili.

Cook for 3 minutes, stirring now and then.

**7** Before you open the rice packages, squeeze to break up any lumps. Pour the rice into the pan.

Stir in the lime juice.

**8** Cook for 2 more minutes, stirring often.

That smells amazing!

STIR

# VARIATIONS

If you want to make this into an entrée, you will need 2 cups of frozen peas or 10oz cooked, peeled shrimp. Add them at the end of step 6 and cook, stirring often, for 2 minutes. Follow the rest of the steps as normal.

# IRENE'S CHICCHE

Hello! I'm Irene and I come from Italy. My recipe is for yummy little dumplings a little like gnocchi, but called "chicche." Ever since I was small, I've been making them with my Nonna (grandmother) at her big kitchen table – sometimes I used to sneak underneath to steal bites of the mixture!

This recipe is for chicche made with spinach and ricotta, served with homemade tomato sauce.

## INGREDIENTS

### For the chicche:

- 10oz frozen chopped spinach
- 1 large egg
- 1½ cups finely grated Parmesan cheese
- 8oz full-fat ricotta cheese
- 2½ cups all-purpose flour
- ¼ teaspoon ground nutmeg
- a pinch of salt

### For the sauce:

- 1 medium onion or 2 shallots
- 2 cloves of garlic
- 1 tablespoon olive oil or other vegetable oil
- a 28oz can of chopped tomatoes
- 10 large basil leaves (optional)
- a pinch of ground black pepper
- 2 pinches of salt

## TIP

Before you start, defrost the spinach – leave at room temperature for a couple of hours, or microwave for 2 minutes on defrost setting.

You will also need a slotted spoon.

38

**1** Squeeze the spinach over a sink to get rid of the water. Put some spinach in a cup. Snip it into pieces, then put them in a big bowl.

Snip the rest of the spinach in the same way.

**2** Crack the egg into a cup – see the instructions on page 7. Put the egg, Parmesan, ricotta, flour, nutmeg and salt in the big bowl.

Mix with your hands until it comes together.

**3** Dust a surface with flour. Split the mixture into four.

Roll each into a thin sausage shape 20 inches long and ¾ inch wide.

ROLL

**4** Snip each sausage into ½ inch pieces. These are your chicche.

Set them aside while you make the sauce.

SNIP

**5** For the sauce, peel the papery skin off the onion and garlic, and slice the onion into small pieces (see page 6).

Crush the garlic.

Garlic crusher

**6** Put the oil in a large frying pan, over medium heat. After 2 minutes, add the onion.

Cook for 2-3 minutes, stirring every now and then, until soft.

**7** Add the garlic and cook for one minute. Pour in the tomatoes and all their juice.

Cook for 10 minutes, stirring now and then.

**8** Tear up the basil leaves. Add them, the pepper and one pinch of salt.

Stir and take the pan off the heat.

**9** Fill a large saucepan two-thirds full with water and put it over high heat.

When the water boils, add a pinch of salt.

**10** Add half the chicche. After about 2 minutes they will bob up to the top. Scoop them out with the slotted spoon.

Put them in the pan with the sauce.

**11** Cook the rest of the chicche in the same way. Then stir the chicche into the sauce.

# VARIATIONS

To make this recipe dairy-free, egg-free, vegan or gluten-free, follow the instructions on page 60.

39

# HERBS AND SPICES

People all around the world flavor food using herbs and spices. Herbs are usually plant leaves or stems, while spices can come from other parts of plants such as seeds, roots or fruits. Many herbs and spices are dried, but some are used fresh.

A spice called **SUMAC** is popular across Western Asian countries such as Turkey, Syria, Palestine, Iraq, Israel and Pakistan. It's made from fruits of the sumac tree, and has a sharp, citrus flavor.

SEEDS

**CILANTRO** has a mild, lemony flavor. Its leaves and stalks are used as an herb, while its small fruits (sometimes called seeds) are a spice known as coriander. It's popular around the world.

*Use it in the recipes on page 30 and 46.*

**TURMERIC** is a spice that comes from the underground stems of a plant from Asia. It has an earthy, slightly bitter taste. It's traditional in Indian, South Asian and Middle Eastern cooking.

POD

**VANILLA** is a spice made from the pods of a flowering orchid plant, which originally came from Central America. Vanilla is used worldwide to give a delicious, mild flavor to sweet foods.

**CHILI** is a spice that comes from hot, spicy fruits known as chili peppers. They first came from South and Central America, and later became popular in traditional Asian and African cooking.

**BASIL** is a leafy herb with a spicy flavor. There are different varieties – "sweet basil" is much loved in Italy, "Thai basil" is used in Southeast Asia, while "holy basil" is popular in India.

*Use sweet basil in the recipe on page 38.*

STAMEN

**SAFFRON** is made from the dried stamens from crocus flowers. It's been used since ancient times in Iran, Greece and Iraq, but is now popular in other parts of the world. It has a smoky flavor and is the most expensive spice.

# MARLEE'S CHOCOLATE CHIP COOKIES

Hi, I'm Marlee and I come from Philadelphia in the U.S.A. For big family get-togethers, I love baking chocolate chip cookies. I learned to make them from my Dad when I was little. We'd bake dozens of them, and load them into the car. When we arrived, the cookies were so popular that family members would sneak them from the pantry and fight over the last one.

> You can use dark or light brown sugar in these cookies – dark makes chewier, more butterscotchy cookies, while light makes crisper cookies.

## INGREDIENTS

- ½ cup (1 stick) butter
- 6 tablespoons granulated sugar
- 6 tablespoons packed brown sugar, either light or dark
- 1 teaspoon vanilla extract
- 1 large egg
- 1 cup + 1 tablespoon all-purpose flour
- a pinch of salt (optional)
- ½ teaspoon baking soda
- ¾ cup chocolate chips

You will also need two large baking trays.

**MAKES 24**

## TIPS

Before you start, leave the butter and egg at room temperature for 30 minutes.

You could use salted butter, and leave out the salt.

**1** Put the butter, both types of sugar and the vanilla in a big bowl. Mix with a spoon, then beat really hard until soft and pale.

You could use an electric mixer.

BEAT

**2** Crack the egg on the rim of a cup. Push your thumbs into the crack. Pull the shell apart so the white and yolk slide into the cup.

Pull out any bits of shell that fall in.

**3** Then, pour the egg into the bowl.

Mix it in.

**4** Put a sieve over a big bowl. Add the flour, salt and baking soda.

Tap so they fall through.

TAP TAP

**5** Mix in gently. Stop as soon as the mixture is smooth. Then, stir in the chocolate chips.

If you can wait, put the bowl in the fridge for 30 minutes – this makes the dough firmer.

Plate

**6** Then, heat the oven to 375°F.

Line the trays – see page 7 for instructions.

Baking paper

**7** Scoop up a tablespoonful of the mixture. Roll it into a ball. Put it on a tray. Keep on doing this until the mixture is used up.

Space the balls well apart as they spread a lot!

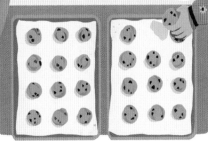

**8** Bake for 10-12 minutes, until golden. Leave on the trays to cool.

Yum!

# VARIATIONS

To make this recipe gluten-free, use gluten-free flour.

To make it dairy-free, use plant-based "butter" from a block and plant-based chocolate chips.

To make it egg-free, replace the egg with 2 tablespoons of plant-based "milk."

To make it vegan, follow the instructions above to make it dairy-free and egg-free.

# KATERYNA'S SYRNYKY PANCAKES

Hi, I'm Kateryna and I grew up in western Ukraine, on my grandparents' farm. Most days my parents left for work early, so my Babcia (grandmother) cooked breakfast for me and my cousin Roman. My favorite was syrnyky (say sear-nee-kee) – little, sweet pancakes. They're delicious topped with strawberry jam and sour cream.

These pancakes contain a fresh, crumbly, tangy cheese we make using milk from our cows.

To make your own syrnyky, you can buy Farmer cheese, or use ordinary cottage cheese.

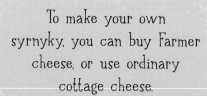

## INGREDIENTS

For the pancakes:

- 2 cups crumbled Farmer cheese, or 2 heaping cups cottage cheese
- 2 tablespoons granulated sugar
- 3 tablespoons all-purpose flour, plus extra for coating
- ½ cup raisins
- sunflower oil or other light cooking oil

Any of these toppings:

- your favorite flavor of jam
- sour cream, heavy cream or yogurt
- a little powdered sugar
- fresh berries

You will also need a large non-stick frying pan.

MAKES AROUND 12

**1** If you're using cottage cheese, spoon it onto a clean cloth dishtowel.

Gather the corners, to enclose the cheese. Squeeze hard over a sink, to get out as much moisture as you can.

*DRIP DRIP DRIP*

**2** Put the Farmer cheese or cottage cheese into a big bowl. Stir in the sugar, flour and raisins.

Spoon some extra flour onto a plate for coating.

**3** Scoop up a tablespoon of the mixture. Tip it onto the flour.

Use floury hands to roll it around until it is coated all over.

*ROLL*

**4** Shape it roughly into a ball, then flatten it so it's as thick as a pencil.

Make more, until the mixture is used up.

**5** Put 1 tablespoon of oil in the pan.

Put it over medium heat for 2-3 minutes.

**6** Carefully put in some pancakes, leaving gaps between. Cook for 2-3 minutes, or until golden-brown underneath.

Peek underneath to see if they're brown.

*SIZZLE*

**7** Turn them over, and cook for 2 minutes more.

**8** Put the pancakes on a plate. Cover with another plate, to keep them warm.

**9** Repeat steps 6 to 8 until all the pancakes are cooked.

Spoon on any toppings just before you eat them.

# VARIATIONS

To make the pancakes dairy-free or vegan, see the instructions on page 61.

To make them gluten-free, use gluten-free flour.

# PRIYA'S SPICED GARBANZOS

Hello, my name is Priya. I'm from South India and my recipe is for chana masala, which means "mixed-spice garbanzos." I have wonderful childhood memories of cooking this with my Paati (grandmother) when I arrived home from school. My sister Aditi and I would eat it with buttered toast on our breezy balcony.

This recipe is quite hot! If you prefer mild flavors, you might want to leave out the green chili and chili powder.

## INGREDIENTS

- 1 onion
- 3 cloves of garlic
- 1 green chili (or more if you like spicy food)
- a 1 inch long piece of fresh ginger
- 3 tablespoons sunflower oil or other light cooking oil
- 1 teaspoon cumin seeds
- a pinch of salt
- 4 tablespoons tomato purée
- 2 teaspoons garam masala spice mix

- 1 teaspoon chana masala spice mix
- 1 teaspoon chili powder (or just 1 pinch if you prefer milder flavors)
- 1½ teaspoons ground coriander
- ½ teaspoon ground turmeric
- 2 x 14oz cans of garbanzo beans
- a small handful of fresh cilantro leaves
- 1 lemon

**1** Take the skin off the onion, then cut the onion into tiny pieces.

The instructions on page 6 will help you.

**2** Peel the papery skin off the garlic.

Crush the garlic.

Garlic crusher

**3** Cut the top off the green chili.

Then, grate the ginger.

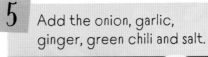

Grater →

Small holes →

**4** Put oil in a large saucepan over medium heat. Add the cumin seeds.

Wait until they start to pop, then turn the heat to low.

POP! POP! POP!

**5** Add the onion, garlic, ginger, green chili and salt.

Cook for 5 minutes, stirring now and then, until the onions are soft and starting to brown.

**6** Add the passata, garam masala, chana masala, chili powder, ground coriander and turmeric.

Cook for 1 minute, stirring all the time.

**7** Pour in the garbanzos and the can liquid. Stir. Turn the heat to medium.

When it starts to bubble, turn the heat to medium/low, and cook for 7 minutes.

**8** Meanwhile, put the cilantro leaves and stalks in a cup.

Snip them up.

Scissors →

**9** Cut the lemon in half.

Squeeze out the juice.

Citrus squeezer

**10** Use a spoon to pull out the green chili.

Stir in the cilantro leaves and the lemon juice, before eating.

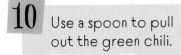

# VARIATIONS

You can buy pre-mixed spices to use in this dish – look for "chana masala" spice mix. If you can't get this, replace it with extra "garam masala" spice mix, which is easy to find.

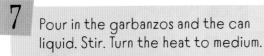

# DANICA'S JAM COOKIES

Hi, I'm Danica and I come from Germany. My recipe is for little cookies with jam in the middle, which I started baking with my Mama and my sister every December when I was a child. We didn't have cookie cutters for them, so each year we hunted for round things to use instead.

If you don't have cookie cutters, use things like a glass and a bottle top...

...but it's easier to use round cookie cutters, if you have them.

## INGREDIENTS

- 1½ cups all-purpose flour
- 1 tablespoon milk
- ¼ cup sugar
- 1 teaspoon vanilla extract
- 1 lemon
- 9 tablespoons butter
- 4 tablespoons jam
- a little powdered sugar, for dusting (optional)

You will also need a large round cutter (around 2 inches across), a small round cutter (around ¾ inch across) and two baking trays.

**MAKES AROUND 20**

**TIP**
Before you start, leave the butter at room temperature for 30 minutes.

**1** Sift the flour through a sieve into a big bowl.

Then add the milk, sugar and vanilla.

**2** Grate the zest from the outside of half the lemon.

Put the zest in the bowl.

Grater

Small holes

**3** Cut the butter into little pieces and put them in the bowl.

**4** Use your hands to squish and mix everything into a lump of dough.

**5** Put in a bowl with a plate on top. Refrigerate for one hour.

**6** Heat the oven to 375°F. Line the trays with baking paper.

See page 7 for help.

**7** Sprinkle a surface and rolling pin with flour. Roll out the dough until it's half as thick as a pencil.

ROLL

**8** Cut out lots of large circles. Use the small cutter to cut holes in the middle of half the circles.

Put the shapes on the trays.

PRESS

**9** Squeeze the scraps together, roll out again and cut more shapes in the same way.

Bake for 10-12 minutes, until golden-brown at the edges.

**10** Lift the cookies onto a cooling rack and leave to cool completely.

Spatula

**11** Spread jam over the whole circles, and then top with the cut-out circles.

You could sift over some powdered sugar.

# VARIATIONS

To make this recipe gluten-free, use gluten-free flour.

To make it dairy-free or vegan, use plant-based "milk" and plant-based "butter" from a block.

You can use any flavor of jam you like. Smooth jams work better.

# COOKING POTS

Soups, stews and other meals cooked in pots are popular in all corners of the globe. Many regions have traditional styles of pots. Here are just some of them.

A clay dish called a **DONABE** is very popular in Japan for cooking stews and noodle soups.

A **BEANPOT** is a clay or metal pot with a lid, traditionally used in the U.S.A. to cook baked beans.

This is a **SUFURIA**, a metal cooking pot used in African countries such as Kenya and Tanzania. It can be big or small, with or without a lid.

In Bulgaria, **GYUVECH** is the name of a pot, and also the type of stew that's cooked in it. Similar pots are used in other countries including Greece, Romania and Turkey.

This is an **OLLA**, used for cooking beans and stews. It's traditional in Spain and Catalonia, as well as in Mexico and parts of the Southwestern U.S.A.

This is a **TAGINE**, used for cooking stews (also called tagines) in North African countries including Morocco and Algeria.

*The recipe on page 52 can be cooked in a tagine.*

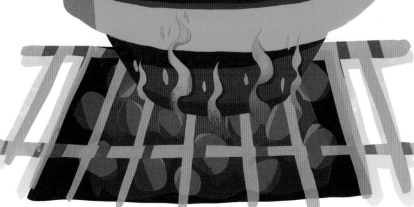

A **HANDI** is a clay or metal pot, used by cooks in North India, Pakistan and Bangladesh. The lid helps to keep food juicy.

## TIP

If you don't have these pots, you can use an ordinary pan instead. The recipe will tell you what to do.

# IKRAM'S KESRA BREAD

Hi, my name is Ikram and I come from Algeria. I learned this recipe from my Mama and Nana (mother and grandmother) when I was younger. It's for a traditional type of flatbread called "kesra" – but thanks to Nana's secret ingredient, our version tastes extra special.

We cook our kesra in the flat base of a cooking pot called a tagine...

...but you can use an ordinary frying pan.

## INGREDIENTS

- 1 cup fine semolina flour
- ½ teaspoon salt
- ½ teaspoon sugar
- 1 package (1¼ teaspoons) active dry yeast
- ⅔ cup warm water
- a little flour, for dusting
- 4 tablespoons (½ stick) butter

**MAKES 4**

You will also need a tagine base or frying pan, preferably non-stick.

**TIP**

Before you start, leave the butter at room temperature for 30 minutes.

52

**1** Mix the semolina, salt, sugar and yeast in a big bowl.

Pour in a little water.

Mix it in with your hands.

**2** Keep on mixing in more water a little at a time, until the mixture clumps into a ball.

You may not need all the water.

**3** Sprinkle a surface with flour. Put the dough on it.

Push the dough away from you, using your knuckles or the heels of your hands.

PUSH

**4** Fold the dough in half towards you...

FOLD

...then push it away again.

Keep on doing this for 5-10 minutes, or until the dough is smooth and springy.

**5** Split it into four.

Pat each into a ball, then roll them until they're circles around 6 inches across.

Rolling pin dusted with flour

**6** Spread the butter over the tops of the circles.

Fold the dough over like this, so the butter is hidden.

The butter is our secret ingredient!

**7** Gently shape each piece into a ball. Roll each one out so it's a 6 inch circle again.

Some butter may squeeze out, but don't worry.

**8** Put a tagine base or frying pan over medium heat for 5 minutes.

Then put in a flatbread.

SIZZLE

**9** Cook for 2-3 minutes, until the bottom has patches of golden-brown.

Flip over and cook the other side for 2-3 minutes.

**10** Cook all the flatbreads in the same way. Leave to cool for a few minutes before eating.

# VARIATIONS

To make this recipe dairy-free or vegan, use plant-based "butter."

To make it gluten-free, replace the semolina with gluten-free flour – see page 61 for instructions.

# BASILE'S PICNIC LOAF

My name is Basile and I'm from France. As a child, every summer
I would visit my aunt, uncle and cousins in the south of France.
We liked to bake this loaf and take it on a hike across lavender
fields or rocky bays, then stop to eat it as we admired the scenery.

**1** Line the pan – see the instructions on page 7. Heat the oven to 350°F.

Baking paper

**2** If necessary, shred the cheese.

Grater

Big holes

**3** Drain the olives in a sieve.

Snip each one in half.

**4** Pat the sun-dried tomatoes with paper towels.

Cut them into small pieces.

SNIP

**5** Run your thumb and first finger along each stalk of thyme, to strip off the leaves.

Hold here

**6** Put the flour, baking powder, salt and pepper in a sieve over a big bowl.

Tap the sieve so everything falls through.

**7** Crack an egg on the rim of a cup. Push your thumbs into the crack. Pull the shell apart so the white and yolk slide into the cup.

Pull out any bits of shell that fall in.

**8** Crack the other eggs in the same way.

Beat to mix the yolks and whites.

Fork

# INGREDIENTS

- 2 cups grated firm cheese such as cheddar
- 1 cup drained pitted black or green olives
- 1 cup drained sun-dried tomatoes from a jar
- a sprig of fresh thyme (optional)
- 2 cups all-purpose flour
- 1 teaspoon baking powder
- a pinch of salt
- a pinch of ground black pepper
- 4 large eggs
- ½ cup milk
- ⅓ cup olive oil
- 1 tablespoon white wine vinegar

You will also need a 6-cup loaf pan measuring around 9x5 inches.

You could replace the olives and/or sun-dried tomatoes with 1 cup of any of the following ingredients:

- fresh cherry tomatoes, snipped into quarters
- preserved bell peppers or artichokes, drained on paper towels and snipped into small pieces

- fresh baby spinach leaves, snipped into small pieces
- nuts such as almonds or walnuts

**9** Pour the eggs, milk, oil and vinegar into the bowl.

Mix well. Don't worry if it looks lumpy.

**10** Stir in the cheese, olives, tomatoes and thyme.

Scrape the mixture into the pan.

PLOP

**11** Bake for 45-50 minutes until a toothpick or skewer comes out clean.

If it doesn't, bake for 10 minutes more, then test again.

**12** Leave in the pan to cool.

To remove the loaf, pull on the ends of the baking paper.

TUG

# VARIATIONS

To make this recipe gluten-free, use gluten-free flour and gluten-free baking powder.

To make it dairy-free, egg-free or vegan, follow the instructions on page 61.

# BEATRIZ'S "BRIGADEIRO" TRUFFLES

I'm Beatriz and I come from Brazil. As a child, for birthday parties and sleepovers I cooked brigadeiros – delicious chocolatey truffles – with Mami (my mom) and my sister Fernanda. Mami stirred everything in the pan, then, when the mixture had cooled, Fernanda and I rolled it into balls.

## INGREDIENTS

- a 14oz can sweetened condensed milk
- 2 tablespoons unsweetened cocoa powder
- 2 tablespoons butter
- chocolate sprinkles, sugar sprinkles or shredded coconut, for coating
- a little sunflower or other light cooking oil

If you're in a hurry for a sweet treat, you can eat the cooled mixture with a spoon!

MAKES AROUND 20

**1** Put the condensed milk, cocoa powder and butter in a large saucepan, over medium-low heat.

Stir with a heat-proof spatula until it bubbles gently.

Turn the heat to low.

**2** Keep stirring for 5 minutes. Pull the spatula along the bottom, to part the mixture. It should take a second to join again. Leave to cool.

If it joins quickly, cook for 2 minutes more then test again.

**3** Pour the coating on a plate. Rub your hands with a little oil. Scoop up half a teaspoon of mixture.

Roll it into a ball, then roll in coating. Then make more.

## VARIATIONS

To make this recipe dairy-free or vegan, follow the instructions on page 61.

# SANDRA'S HOT CHOCOLATE

Hi, my name is Sandra and I'm from Galicia, in Spain. This is my family recipe for hot chocolate – but it's much thicker and richer than most hot chocolate. I have childhood memories of eating it at New Year as a dipping sauce for crispy snacks called churros.

I love the rich taste of the semi-sweet chocolate in this recipe, but use milk chocolate if you prefer..

You could make this hot chocolate for dipping little cookies or fruit, or eat it with a spoon!

## INGREDIENTS

- 1 cup milk
- 4oz semi-sweet chocolate
- 1½ tablespoons cornstarch

**MAKES 4 LITTLE CUPS**

**1** Set aside 2 tablespoons of the milk in a measuring cup.

Put the rest in a pan over medium heat.

**2** When the milk steams, turn down the heat to low. Break in the chocolate. Stir until it's melted.

Take the pan off the heat.

**3** Mix the cornstarch into the milk in the cup. Pour this mixture into the pan, stirring all the time.

You may need a hand!

**4** Keep stirring all the time, until it becomes really thick.

Then pour into little cups or bowls.

POUR

## VARIATIONS

To make this recipe dairy-free or vegan, use plant-based "milk" and plant-based chocolate.

# SWAPPING INGREDIENTS

All the recipes in this book are vegetarian, but you can make them vegan, nut-free, gluten-free, dairy-free, egg-free (or any combination of these) using the instructions that follow. If you're cooking for someone with special dietary requirements, always check packaged ingredients such as flour, baking powder, sugar, spreads or sugar sprinkles, in case they contain anything unsuitable.

## SUNHA'S ZUCCHINI PANCAKES

- To make this recipe GLUTEN-FREE, replace the flour with gluten-free flour and the soy sauce with gluten-free "tamari" sauce.

- The dipping sauce is spicy – you can leave out the chili, or eat the pancakes without any sauce.

## EMINE'S KISIR SALAD

- To make this recipe GLUTEN-FREE, replace the bulgur wheat or couscous with the same amount of quinoa. Skip step 1 and put the quinoa in a pan, add 4½ cups of water, turn the heat to medium and wait until the water boils, then turn down the heat so it's just bubbling and cook for 15 minutes, or until the water disappears. Then, take it off the heat and leave for 15 minutes. Follow steps 2-7. Put the quinoa in a big bowl, then add the other ingredients at step 8. Follow the rest of the steps as normal.

## BECKY'S BOUREKAS

- To make this recipe GLUTEN-FREE, use gluten-free puff pastry and gluten-free flour for dusting at step 7.

- To make it EGG-FREE, replace the egg with 2 tablespoons of milk or plant-based "milk."

- To make it DAIRY-FREE, use plant-based "milk" and plant-based pastry, and replace the feta with an additional small potato, 2 cloves of garlic, 1 onion and 2 tablespoons of olive oil. At step 1 use both potatoes; after step 3, chop the onion and crush the garlic (see page 6) then put the oil, onion and garlic in a pan over medium heat and cook for 5 minutes, stirring every now and then; at step 5 mix the onion and garlic into the mashed potato with the pepper.

- To make it VEGAN, follow the instructions above to make it dairy-free and egg-free.

- If you want to avoid SESAME, leave out the seeds.

# ELON & OKKIE'S NEW YEAR COOKIES

- To make this recipe GLUTEN-FREE, use gluten-free flour.

- If you want to avoid SESAME, replace the sesame seeds with the same amount of granulated sugar or unsweetened shredded coconut.

# RUTH'S MILK & HONEY PUDDING

- To make this recipe GLUTEN-FREE, top with raspberries or gluten-free ginger snap cookies.

- To make it DAIRY-FREE, leave out the milk and cream and instead use 2 cups coconut milk or plant-based "cream" and top with raspberries or plant-based ginger snap cookies.

- To make it VEGAN, make it dairy-free, as above and replace the honey with maple syrup or agave syrup.

# SHARON'S "RED RED" PEAS

- This recipe is already gluten-free, egg-free, dairy-free, vegan and nut-free.

# ELLIOT'S MIDSUMMER CAKE

- To make this recipe GLUTEN-FREE, use gluten-free flour and gluten-free baking powder.

- To make it EGG-FREE, leave out the eggs and instead use 6 tablespoons sunflower oil and 12 tablespoons water. Skip step 2 and instead put 3 tablespoons of the oil, 6 tablespoons of the water and ½ teaspoon of the vanilla in a measuring cup and mix. Follow step 3 to sift the dry ingredients into the bowl, then pour in the oil and water mixture before stirring gently until just mixed. Follow the rest of the steps as normal.

- To make it DAIRY-FREE, for the frosting, use plant-based "cream cheese" and plant-based whippable "cream."

- To make it VEGAN, make it egg-free and dairy-free as above.

# PAMELA'S FRUIT SALAD

- To make this recipe DAIRY-FREE or VEGAN, leave out the sauce, or use plant-based condensed "milk" and plain plant-based Greek-style "yogurt."

# VIC & ABI'S ICE-CREAM

- To make this recipe DAIRY-FREE or VEGAN, use plant-based condensed "milk" and plant-based whippable "cream."

## IRENE'S CHICCHE

- To make this recipe GLUTEN-FREE, use gluten-free flour.

- To make it EGG-FREE, replace the egg with 4 tablespoons of water.

- To make it DAIRY-FREE, replace the Parmesan with plant-based "Parmesan" or 6 tablespoons of nutritional yeast and replace the ricotta with extra-firm tofu crumbled finely.

- To make it VEGAN, make it egg-free and dairy-free as above.

## JACOB'S ROLLED EGGS

- To make this recipe GLUTEN-FREE, use a gluten-free wrap.

- To make it EGG-FREE, leave out the eggs and instead use 1 cup chickpea flour, a pinch of turmeric and 1 cup water. After step 4, put the chickpea flour and turmeric in a bowl and whisk in a little of the water; add the rest of the water a little at a time, whisking each time, then follow the rest of the steps as normal, using plant-based mayonnaise for the dipping sauce.

- To make it VEGAN, make it egg-free as above and use a plant-based wrap.

## GEMMA'S COCONUT BARFI

- To make this recipe DAIRY-FREE, replace the condensed milk with plant-based condensed "milk," and use plant-based spread.

- To make it VEGAN, make it dairy-free as above, and decorate with plant-based sprinkles or pistachios.

- To make it NUT-FREE, decorate with sprinkles instead of pistachios.

## ISLA & OLIVE'S FRIED RICE

- To make this into a MAIN DISH, you will need 2 cups frozen peas or 10oz cooked, peeled shrimp: add them at the end of step 6 and cook, stirring often, for 2 minutes, then follow the rest of the steps as normal.

- To make this variation VEGETARIAN or VEGAN, use the peas.

## MARLEE'S CHOCOLATE CHIP COOKIES

- To make this recipe GLUTEN-FREE, use gluten-free flour.

- To make it EGG-FREE, skip step 2 and replace the egg with 2 tablespoons of plant-based "milk," added at step 3.

- To make it DAIRY-FREE, use plant-based "butter" from a block, and plant-based chocolate chips.

- To make it VEGAN, make it egg-free and dairy-free as above.

# KATERYNA'S SYRNYKY PANCAKES

- To make this recipe GLUTEN-FREE, use gluten-free flour.
- To make it DAIRY-FREE or VEGAN, leave out the cheese and instead use ¾ pacakge firm tofu (1½ cups), 2 tablespoons plant-based "yogurt" and 1 tablespoon lemon juice. At steps 1 and 2, squeeze and crumble the tofu instead of the cheese; at step 2 add the "yogurt" and lemon juice along with the other ingredients. Follow the rest of the steps as normal.

# PRIYA'S SPICED GARBANZOS

- This recipe is already gluten-free, egg-free, dairy-free, vegan and nut-free.

# DANICA'S JAM COOKIES

- To make this recipe GLUTEN-FREE, use gluten-free flour.
- To make it DAIRY-FREE or VEGAN, use plant-based "milk" and plant-based "butter" from a block.

# IKRAM'S KESRA BREAD

- To make this recipe GLUTEN-FREE, replace the semolina flour with gluten-free flour, and at step 4, knead the dough for just 1 or 2 minutes until smooth.
- To make it DAIRY-FREE or VEGAN, use plant-based "butter."

# BASILE'S PICNIC LOAF

- To make this recipe GLUTEN-FREE, use gluten-free flour.
- To make it EGG-FREE, leave out the eggs and milk and instead use ⅔ cup plain, unsweetened plant-based "yogurt." Skip steps 7 and 8 and at step 9, add the "yogurt," oil and vinegar and mix. Follow the rest of the steps as normal.
- To make it DAIRY-FREE, replace the milk with plant-based "milk" and replace the cheese with 8 tablespoons of nutritional yeast, by skipping step 2 and adding the yeast at step 10.
- To make it VEGAN, make it egg-free as above and replace the cheese with 8 tablespoons of nutritional yeast, by skipping step 2 and adding the yeast at step 10.

# BEATRIZ'S "BRIGADEIRO" TRUFFLES

- To make this recipe DAIRY-FREE or VEGAN, use plant-based condensed "milk," plant-based "butter" and coat with plant-based sprinkles or shredded coconut.

# SANDRA'S HOT CHOCOLATE

- To make this recipe DAIRY-FREE or VEGAN, use plant-based "milk" and plant-based chocolate.

# INDEX

# ACKNOWLEDGEMENTS

Huge thanks to the following people and their families who have kindly given permission for their recipes to be included in this book.

ZUCCHINI PANCAKES, pages 10-11 – Sunha Park
KISIR SALAD, pages 12-13 – Emine Ülkü Şimşek
BOUREKAS, pages 16-17 – Becky Walker
NEW YEAR COOKIES, pages 18-19 – Helen Lee
MILK & HONEY PUDDING, pages 20-21 – Ruth Brocklehurst
"RED RED" PEAS, pages 24-25 – Sharon Kukubor-Tay
MIDSUMMER CAKE, pages 26-27 – Linda Essen-Möller
FRUIT SALAD, page 28 – Pamela Katic
ICE-CREAM, page 29 – Abigail Wheatley
ROLLED EGGS, pages 30-31 – Senti Mukasa
COCONUT BARFI, pages 34-35 – Gemma Baijnath
FRIED RICE, pages 36-37 – Kimberley Kinloch
CHICCHE, pages 38-39 – Irene Olivo
CHOCOLATE CHIP COOKIES, pages 42-43 – Marlee Newman
SYRNYKY PANCAKES, pages 44-45 – Kateryna Mokra
SPICED GARBANZOS, pages 46-47 – Chaaya Prabhat
JAM COOKIES, pages 48-49 – Danica Utermöhlen
KESRA BREAD, pages 52-53 – Ikram Belaid
PICNIC LOAF, pages 54-55 – Basile Brosse
"BRIGADEIRO" TRUFFLES, page 56 – Beatriz Liberatti
HOT CHOCOLATE, page 57 – Sandra Gomez Perez

**SERIES EDITOR:** Jane Chisholm    **SERIES DESIGNER:** Zoe Wray

Additional design by Eleanor Stevenson & Vickie Robinson

With thanks to Kathy Kordalis